TO MY DAUGHTER

Words of Wisdom On Your Wedding Day

MONICA JACKSON

To My Daughter: Words of Wisdom on Your Wedding Day

Requests may be sent to: MonicaJackson@trimarriage.com or www.TriMarriage.com

Published by Monica Jackson
TriMarriage Publishing

Library of Congress Control Number: 2021912215
ISBN 978-1-63877-620-8 (softcover)
ISBN 978-1-63877-621-5 (eBook)

Editor: Susan Harbin
Cover Design: Anthony J. Jackson
Interior Design: Praditha Kahatapitiya
Author Photo: Anthony J. Jackson

Printed in the United States of America 2021 First Edition

To Jamoni, Jamaya, Toni Lynn, Kaitlyn, and Allison

— my own five daughters! It was my love for you, along with my passion to see marriages thrive in general, that has inspired me to write this book! May you follow God's purposes for your lives, wherever they may lead you!

Love,
Mommy

Table of Contents

Foreword 1

Preface 5

Introduction 9

Build Your House 15

Build Intimacy 23

Build Mutual Respect 35

Build Open, Effective Communication 47

Build Your Prayer Life 65

Work On Yourself 77

It's Not All About You 85

Your Body Is Not Your Own 97

Have Beauty On Lock 107

Let Joy Thrive In Your Heart 117

Conclusion 127

Reflections 131

Appendix: A List of Other Resources 135

Acknowledgements 137

Foreword

by Jamoni A. Davis

Living with them, as the eldest of Anthony and Monica Jackson's five daughters, I never thought that my mom and stepdad's relationship was perfect, but it was definitely ideal in my eyes. Marriage, alone, is hard. Add on two kids from a previous marriage, and you can imagine the obstacles they had to tackle. I commend (despite how annoying I often found it as a child) how they always presented a united front, admire their teamwork and collaboration, as well as their sense of camaraderie.

Today, what I love seeing and truly appreciate is their growth. As children, our parents often try to protect and hide us from as many "unseemly" things as possible. Sometimes, these things include parts of themselves, like their temperament, struggles or past. We find them putting on a "parent front." Yet, we can't hide from those we are constantly around and we are robbing others and ourselves of the opportunity of community. One of the devil's biggest tools is isolation and the ability to make us believe that our problems are ours alone, or that we should hide and pretend in shame. God calls us to live in the light. To accept our truth so we may heal and live out His purpose to bring others to Him. To know that we are not alone.

Having been "raised" in the church, I always say that before I knew God for myself, I knew Him through the testimonies of others. Through the testimonies of my family, I came to understand that if I did what they did and listened to The Lord, everything in life would be more than ok.

Watching my parents grow to be the people they are today, and to have the relationship they have today, was my ultimate testimony leading into my marriage.

Coming into my third year of marriage, this book has led to my own testimonies.

When Armand proposed, though I had no idea what I was getting into (who can?), I felt having multiple examples of healthy, lasting marriages in my life gave me somewhat of a decent foundation for my new role.

Once word got out, we got TONS of advice from any and everyone who could catch our ear. I remember most of it being directed towards me. While Armand's advice was primarily "happy wife, happy life" type stuff (which sounds good to ME, but what does that even really MEAN?). Marriage counseling, though it did get us to face and think about some things, wasn't very thorough. So I was really looking forward to this so-called book my mom said she'd give to me to prepare to be a wife.

It didn't help that MY parents ran the marriage ministry at our church. I think I was looking for something that would lay it out for me. Something close to an index of issues and their associated solutions. So, when the hubby was doing "xyz," I could just remember chapter 8 and, boom. Problem solved.

Of course, nothing in life works like that. But you know what? This kind of does.

Walking down the aisle, testimony in hand, I found I had no real idea of how to apply what I had seen with my parents. I quickly realized that we weren't them and seemed to have a new set of issues. While I never understood my parents to be perfect, I felt like they couldn't help with a lot of what I was going through and experiencing. MY problems were so much worse and it didn't help that sometimes it seemed I was the only one trying to do things right. There were plenty of times I felt things were too screwed up to be fixed and that I should just "start over." Technically, that worked for my mom, right? I thought that, maybe, I should "heal more" on my own instead of continuing to subject my family to my issues. In utilizing the advice given in this book, I'm truly understanding how The Lord is the God of REDEMPTION. That He works in the midst of the mess, not in spite of it. Just like we aren't to fall despondent over our sinful nature, God wasn't calling me to hanker over the past and a do-over but to lean on Him. So He could show me HIS power! No matter how far gone my situation felt, or who's "fault" it was, I found that when I focused on things like; building my house and simply working on myself; The Lord was doing the rest of the heavy lifting. Whether it be changing my attitude or my husband's perspective on something, I took it to God and saw Him WORK and TRANSFORM.

No marriage is the same. We all have our own set of details on where things may go wrong. And I'm definitely not implying these are "quick" or even easy solutions for having the "perfect" marriage. What I have found within these pages are critical ways to reflect on myself and my specific impact on my union with my husband. I found that God honors a marriage done the right way and there are promises for us specifically when we obey His Word.

So, when I say that this works pretty much like the index I was looking for, I mean that, at the end of the day, God tells us how to live life. He never promises that life will be easy and stress-free once we accept Him, but He does promise COMFORT and PEACE in understanding HE is in control of it ALL, if we surrender it. That He loves us and knows what's best.

As you follow these pages, I pray that ultimately, you feel comforted and know that God is already doing the work in your marriage. All He ever asks for, to do his work, is a WILLING spirit. Your picking this up tells me you have some of that. Just like it only takes for you to have the faith of a mustard seed to move mountains, He will use WHATEVER will you have to give Him, if you'll surrender it.

Preface

When my daughter told me that her boyfriend had proposed marriage to her, and she said yes, I was so excited for her! But in that same moment, I realized that it would be so good if she could have a better understanding of marriage and how to approach it than I had when I got married. I am blessed to have a beautiful marriage relationship with my husband, but a lot went into building this relationship, and I wasn't sure what or how much my kids understood about it. There was plenty I had to learn on the fly because I didn't know much myself initially. I made mistakes and thankfully learned from them, making adjustments along the way. I learned the right and wrong ways of working through disagreements and conflict, and how to fight fair and productively. Though struggle in marriage is a given — anytime you bring two people together from different backgrounds and upbringings, there's going to be some friction — I didn't want my daughter to be as caught off guard and unprepared for marriage as I was. I felt a responsibility to pass on to her what I'd learned so far. So, I wrote what turned out to be a devotional for her.

We intended to have it in our daughter's hands by her wedding day, but life threw a lot at us in the nine months between the conception of the idea and that day. My family was invited to fly out to LA to be on Family Feud, so we had to prepare for that; we threw my mom a big 70th birthday bash with only two months to plan; my father passed away unexpectedly as the rest of us were on our way to LA, one month before my daughter's wedding day — and that's when everything just came to a screeching halt! After that, all kinds of discouragement kept me from writing. Then, The Lord led me to a ministry training program He used to provide me with much-needed clarity on my life, and put me on a road towards healing. After this, and around the time of our family's rescheduled trip to the Family Feud (just over a year later), God reminded me to finish the book for my daughter. After we returned from LA, I got right on it and had it printed and into her hands one year, one month and two days after her wedding. Once I got it printed and picked it up, The Lord immediately gave me more to write. Normally, this would make me kick myself that I didn't hold off a little longer, so more would've been included in what I gave my daughter, but this time, I understood that I had to do the original thing that God led me to do before He was going to move me on to the next phase.

For a long time, Anthony and I have had a heart to affect as many people as possible with the message that God's design for marriage really does work. With that, and the feeling of being nudged by God, we decided that I would rewrite the devotional, and publish it to share with many brides. All this has shown me that God's plan will prevail no matter what is going on in life! Philippians 2:13

says, "for it is God who works in you to will and to act in order to fulfill his good purpose." (NIV)

So, it is out of obedience to God, His guidance, and often His carrying me through this process, that I present this book to you, bathed in much prayer, that it will affect your life as well as your marriage in a transitional way.

Introduction

No Slackers!

Marriage is hard!

I'm gonna just let that linger here for a moment… If you don't believe me, ask any couple married for two years or longer. Whether they are settling into a nice groove or are struggling every step of the way, they will all tell you the same thing: "This ain't easy!"

Marriage is work. Especially on the front end. There's no "…and they both lived happily ever after…" apart from some consistent effort. I feel it is very important to get an understanding of that in the beginning. The sooner, the better. I see engaged or newlywed couples all the time that believe their loving feelings for one another will blaze a smooth path for their marriage. They have the fairytale wedding, go on a beautiful honeymoon, come back to their new home and life together, open all those gifts… and somewhere after that, the bottom drops out. Reality creeps in and that smooth road they thought they could just cruise down towards their 'happily ever after' is bumpy — rocky, even. There are obstructions. Things just aren't falling into place. We as married couples need to seek God, as He is the architect of marriage (Genesis 2:18-25), who gives us the instruction and grace we need to succeed in it.

Movies and television will have us believe that if we have "loving feelings in our heart" for our spouse, then our marriage will magically work out. That cannot be further from the truth. In the Bible love is an action word:

> John 21:16 —"He said to him a second time, "Simon, son of John, do you love me?... *Tend my sheep*.""
>
> John 14:15 — "If you love me, you will *keep my commandments*"
>
> John 3:16 — "For God so loved the world that *He gave His only Son*..."
>
> Romans 5:8 — "God *demonstrates* His own love toward us, in that while we were yet sinners, Christ died for us."

Throughout the Bible and in our lives, God qualifies His love for us by His actions. He requires us to reciprocate, and He expects no less from our relationships with one another. We are expected to show love — not just feel it. Look at I Corinthians 13:4a, which says, "Love is patient and kind..." You see that? Patient and kind are action words. You have to *do* those to show love. Then verse 7 takes it further: "Love bears all things, believes all things, hopes all things, endures all things." Bears, believes, hopes, and endures... all things?? That's some deep stuff!

Good marriage relationships are built... they don't just happen. They are built over time, and as they endure different situations and circumstances, they grow stronger. There will be times when you don't feel so lovey towards your husband. Understanding and learning how to make your decisions based on a purpose higher than how you currently feel will carry you through these times, allowing your marriage to survive long enough for you to move into a better space with your husband.

When making a stew, you put in the main ingredients (meat, veggies, broth, herbs, seasonings, etc.) and let them simmer for a couple of hours to let the flavors develop. This is the first step in melding your ingredients. But after eating the stew for dinner the first day, putting it in the refrigerator overnight, then reheating it for dinner the next day, it will taste even better! As the ingredients spend even more time together in the cold of the fridge, the flavors 'marry' or combine more efficiently.

Your marriage relationship is similar to the stew: As the heat is turned up in your relationship, or as you encounter various types of settings together that may be uncomfortable, difficult or intense, you grow closer together. As things cool down in your marriage, you learn to live with one another and love each other without things being so hot and heavy, or exciting all of the time. You learn to love intentionally instead of loving according to how you're feeling in the moment. Through many shared experiences, God makes you into a 'new dish'. This new dish is different from the original main ingredients were on their own. It has a better flavor, with greater potency. It has varied textures. You can detect the flavors of the original ingredients, but they have been elevated by one another. This is the essence of my prayer for your marriage:

"For this reason, ever since I heard about your faith in the Lord Jesus and your love for all God's people, I have not stopped giving thanks for you, remembering you in my prayers. I keep asking that the God of our Lord Jesus Christ, the glorious Father, may give you the Spirit of wisdom and revelation, so that you may know him better. I pray that the eyes of your heart may be enlightened in order that you may know the hope to which he has called you, the riches of his glorious inheritance in his holy people, and his incomparably great power for us who believe. That power is the same as the mighty strength he exerted when he raised Christ from the dead and seated him at his right hand in the heavenly realms, far above all rule and authority, power and dominion, and every name that is invoked, not only in the present age but also in the one to come." — Ephesians 1:15-21

For every bride that purchases this book, I thank God for her marriage, and I pray that she will be open to God, that He will open her eyes to who He is, His hand in her life, and that His intentions for her are goodness. I pray that He gives her wisdom to navigate the nuances of her unique relationship with her husband, within the guides He has, and to know that she can have a great marriage if she looks to the Author of marriage (God). That she comes to understand the value of her position as a wife to her husband, her family, and before God — a special calling He has equipped her for, will always help her with, and that has the potential to make a huge impact in this world.

The layout of this book: You will notice that the titles of the first five chapters of this book begin with the word "build." This is because these are the five building blocks for the foundation of your marriage. They are practical tools you can put into practice. The last five chapters are more about your state of being (or mind) for you to have a healthy marriage. They support the first five chapters. You will also see that some topics are touched on in other chapters. This is because each subject addressed in this book is related to the others in some way. Taking all of the themes into account will make you balanced. You can work on what you feel you need to work on in parts, with the goal being that you eventually absorb and address everything that's covered here.

At the end of each section, there is at least one question with room for you to write your thoughts (sometimes a second question will follow the previous question). Take time after reading each section to ponder the question(s) in light of what was discussed, and jot down what comes to mind.

If you're just about to get married, or are a newlywed (in your first year of marriage), you will benefit from reading this twice. Reading this at the very beginning of your marriage journey will help you form a healthy perspective as you embark on this new season of life. In about a year or two after, reread this as a refresher to evaluate the progress of your marriage and make necessary notes and adjustments based on your actual experiences.

If you've already been married for a while, don't feel that it's too late for you to read this book! Every day you wake up on this earth is a great day for you to try something new, do what's right, and/or bring about some change for good in your life! Visit our website and take The Marriage Test in addition to reading this book (see appendix).

Whatever your station, go into your marriage submitted to God, and ready to put in the work. Be intentional about *building* your marriage relationship with your new husband. Marriage may be hard, but it will be worth the effort!

Build Your House

Charm is deceitful, and beauty is passing, but a woman who fears the LORD, she shall be praised.
— Proverbs 31:30 (NKJV)

Young daughter of God, I am sure that you are beautiful to look at! You know how to accentuate your feminine features! You are some combination of fun, funny, caring, thoughtful, loving, witty, knowledgeable, ambitious, adventurous, kind, and spontaneous! You may know how to use your charms to bend your husband to your will, or you may even have the ability to cause your husband to melt in the palm of your hand. Nothing is wrong with any of that. In fact, these are great qualities that help you get along in this world. I'm sure your husband took note of all this, and more, as he fell in love with you. But going forward, and particularly in your marriage, you need to make sure that you're a woman who fears the Lord above all else.

This is what I like to call one of those 'bottom line' items. When things aren't going well in your marriage (and this WILL happen), when you're angry at each other, when you can't agree, when you don't like each other, or one of you doesn't like the other, no amount of 'cute,' charm or beauty can keep you together, or your marriage on track. You MUST be a woman who fears the Lord. **Proverbs 9:10** states, *"The fear of the Lord is the beginning of wisdom, and the knowledge of the Holy One is understanding."* (NASB) Being a woman who fears the Lord will help you make wise decisions in the face of difficult situations you will certainly encounter in your marriage: heartbreak; sorrow; being misunderstood; not being considered; not being heard; playing second fiddle; baby blues; frustration; etc. It will also help you make the right decisions during awesome highs: victories, personal fulfillment, promotions, new babies, increases in finances, homeownership, having worked through and resolved a tough issue plaguing your marriage for years, etc. My favorite stanza in C. T. Studd's famous poem1[1] is:

"Give me Father, a purpose deep,
In joy or sorrow Thy word to keep;
Faithful and true what e'er the strife,
Pleasing Thee in my daily life;
Only one life, twill soon be past,
Only what's done for Christ will last."

[1] *Only One Life, poem by Charles Thomas Studd*

Marriage is for the rest of your life here on earth. You must have your eye on the long game, not just the here and now. The decisions you make in your marriage, and how you act toward your husband, will affect your relationship in the future, one way or the other.

Proverbs 14:1 has been very impacting for me, in how I viewed my role in my own marriage. It says, *"The wise woman builds her house, but the foolish tears it down with her own hands."* (NASB) In the throes of a heated argument, the Spirit still whispers to me based on this verse: *Don't be the foolish woman who tears down her house with her own hands*. When I came across this verse, I was that foolish woman. I could see it in my husband's eyes every time I pridefully snapped and said something demeaning, in the name of 'being right.' I could see it in my children's eyes when I droned on and on in a lecture. Too much of what I was bringing to the table was hurtful and not very helpful. I was tearing down and discouraging the people in our house with my words. This was an eye opener for me. Before running across this passage, I didn't understand the power I had in my marriage: That I can *choose*. I can build, or I can tear down, but the choice is mine. I am challenging you to choose for yourself, today, to be the wise woman who BUILDS her house.

What do I mean when I say, "build your house?" I'm calling for you to INVEST in your marriage by investing in your husband. Build him up. Show him you respect him. Make it a habit of telling him what you admire and appreciate about him, so that when you have a little constructive criticism, he can be open to hear you, instead of it just sounding like everything else that comes out of your mouth about him: negativity, put-downs, and more negativity. Don't be a 'smarty pants.' Who cares what you know if you're being condescending and/or trying to shove it down his throat. Present your viewpoints with love and respect, but be willing to submit to his leadership even if he goes another route. Give him room to fail as he is on his own journey of growth. Don't feel like you have to follow up every one of his botched decisions with an "I told you so…" speech. Be willing to respectfully and honestly communicate how you feel. Don't assume that he should know anything that you have not already told him, and speak to him in a way that you would want him to speak to you.

And then… Watch. God. WORK!

I promise you, He will! You just have to put your trust in HIM and what the Bible says. Don't put it in your own knowledge, or what others tell you that is contrary to what God says. Don't put it in your emotions: Never trust in your emotions alone, but use them as a gauge. Always compare what you feel with the facts and truth, or they will mislead you! Don't put your trust in your husband's love for you. It's gonna let you down one day. Put your trust in God and God ONLY, as you figure out and do the things you can do to deposit into your marriage.

I used to believe that I had to figure out how to get my husband to understand how to see things my way, when I felt I had a better understanding than him. After a lot of frustrating conversations over several years of marriage, I came to see that a lot of my striving was in vain. There were just certain things that Anthony had to learn his own way. And sometimes, he had to bump his head many times for it to really sink in. But when it did, it was miraculous! And we looked backed on the situation and realized there were other things he picked up along the way, besides the goal I had in mind! God orchestrated all of that!

You may know this very familiar verse, but don't 'yada, yada' it as you read it today. REALLY soak up what it's saying to you:

> ***Proverbs 3:5-8*** *– "Trust in the Lord with all your heart and do not lean on your own understanding. In all your ways acknowledge Him, and He will make your paths straight. Do not be wise in your own eyes; fear the Lord and turn away from evil. It will be healing to your body and refreshment to your bones." (NASB)*

How much of your heart does this passage tell you to trust God with? In how many of your ways (or the things you do) does it tell you to acknowledge (or look to) God? The answer to both of those questions is ALL. Just let that marinate for a moment…

Now, I want you to circle the things these verses tell you TO do. Put an X on the things they tell you NOT to do. Highlight the things that the verses say WILL HAPPEN because of following the advice in them. Like all instructional scripture, this passage is not just a cool little adage to put on a desk or decorate your walls with, but it is meant to be put into *practice* — and still be put on your desk and decorate your walls with— but as a reminder of how you are to *live* your life. We must be *intentional* about how we conduct ourselves in our daily lives, or we will live to regret being so careless. Great marriages are *built*. They don't just happen because you love each other so much, know so much Bible scripture, are such good people, or are so well suited for one another. My prayer for your marriage is that you will FEAR THE LORD, take His advice, and be like the wise woman who BUILDS HER HOUSE.

What can you start or stop doing *today* to build your house? Write it down in detail.

Build Intimacy

"'For this reason a man will leave his father and mother and be united to his wife, and the two will become one flesh.' So they are no longer two, but one flesh. Therefore what God has joined together, let no one separate."
– Mark 10:7-9 (KJV)

D*ivorce* is a dirty word that should never be uttered between a husband and wife. When you get married, whether you realize it or not, you stand before God and witnesses and vow *'till death do us part'*. And if you respect God enough to know who He is, you already should understand why you don't want to break a vow to Him.

When we use the "D-word" in marriage (divorce), it goes against what the Bible commands of us. **Ephesians 5:22** says, *"Wives, submit to your own husbands, as to the*

Lord." (ESV) You can't be in submission to your husband if you are throwing in his face that you *'don't have to be here'*, or you *'don't need him'*, or however you may say it. **Ephesians 5:28-30** says,

> *"In the same way husbands should love their wives as their own bodies. He who loves his wife loves himself. For no one ever hated his own flesh, but nourishes and cherishes it, just as Christ does the church, because we are members of his body."* (ESV)

A husband cannot be one who loves his wife as his own body if he seems to have one foot out the door. If his wife can't be secure in his love for her because he has made it known that he may not stick around if certain circumstances persist, or if particular demands aren't met, then he's not cherishing her. Just the mention of this word can undermine any intimacy or security in your marriage. If there's a chance your husband might leave, then how could you ever be completely open and transparent with him? If you make it known you may not stay with your husband, how can he trust you enough to be vulnerable and transparent with you? Intimacy in marriage is built over time. Throwing the 'D-word' around subverts any efforts towards it.

Using the 'D-word' isn't the only way we can sabotage our marriages. We also do it when we reserve or hold back part of ourselves - or information, or finances - we aren't willing to share, to protect ourselves in case the marriage doesn't work. We have to be 'All In' like the 2016 Cleveland Cavaliers, to have a successful marriage. My husband and I call it "Loving Without Reserve." You must have a made-up mind you will be fully committed to one another. This is definitely how God sees marriage:

> *"He answered, "Have you not read that he who created them from the beginning made them male and female, and said, 'Therefore a man shall leave his father and his mother and hold fast to his wife, and the two shall become one flesh'? So they are no longer two but one flesh. What therefore God has joined together, let not man separate.""*
> **– Matthew 19:4-6 (ESV)**

Now, this may sound radical for a twenty-first-century woman, but I believe that this verse shows that you must be willing to lose your identity to an extent. I've often heard people say of marriage, "I've lost myself..." or "Make sure you hold on to your identity, girl!" I don't believe that clinging to an identity of your own —particularly the one you had before you got married — is in line with what the Bible teaches, or healthy for marriage. In Matthew 19 above, the Bible speaks of '*two becoming one flesh*'. This signifies that during marriage, two people come together in such a way that they make a new, unique personality. When God brings a man and a woman together, He is doing a new thing! It says, "*So they are no longer two but one flesh.*" This does not mean that you have to cease reaching for desires and goals you have, or had, as a single woman. Nor do I believe it means you have to throw yourself into anyone's 'mold' of a wife, or completely into your husband's goals or agenda, leaving all yours behind. It's just that you don't have to pursue your goals or interests all on your own with your own knowledge, your own resources, your own timing. This is good news! A married couple should consistently discuss their individual life objectives and intentions, as they seek The Lord, all the while collaborating on some 'goals of the union' – so to speak – to work toward side by side. There may be some seasons of life where you will seem to play more of a supportive role, as your husband is actively working towards something, and then there will be seasons where you will have a more active role, and your husband will be in a place of assistance and encouragement. In addition, you'll have seasons where you're both working on your personal goals, while encouraging and supporting one another. And then there will be super-cool times where you will work, side by side, in collaboration with one another toward a shared goal! This is also why it is so important to spend time with your husband, doing things you love to do together, as well as some things that just he enjoys, and vice versa.

So, instead of putting all of your focus on your own individual efforts, endeavors, or even feelings, invest in some 'us-related activities.' Be sure to take interest in your husband's passions, particularly those that may not necessarily appeal to you. This is one way you can communicate that you love your husband and plan to be with him for the long haul. It is also a great way to get to know him even better! We come to a deeper understanding of one another when we not only know what they like to do, but have taken the time to experience and understand what they appreciate about it. You may come to actually regard it on some level yourself!

My husband is into automobiles and working with his hands. He LOVES to watch shows on building cars and motorbikes on television. That has never been my choice of entertainment, but we enjoy spending time together, so I would watch his shows along with him. We used to watch shows like Monster Garage, Overhaulin', Orange County Choppers, etc. As we watched, he would point out what he found cool, explain some things about what was going on or tools being used, or share stories of his experiences on a similar undertaking (he used to be an automotive technician). Eventually, I began to respect, and even admire, the skills that these craftsmen had, and the art of their profession. I enjoyed watching these shows with him, and it gave us more stuff to talk about. Now, his guy friends weren't the only ones he could discuss episodes of his favorite shows with. He could share his excitement and joy over them with me! And I could understand what he was talking about, and be honestly interested in his opinions about it. This brought us closer as a couple. It was another facet of himself that he could share with me, and that I had fully accepted. I could tell this delighted him! Had I not shown any interest — had I chosen not to be bothered with this passion of his — that would translate to him as my rejection of this part of him. And when people feel rejected, they put up walls, while on the other hand, when they feel accepted, they are more comfortable. They are more likely to open up to you about deeper things. They let the walls down. This is very important for marital intimacy:

We must establish an atmosphere in our marriages where walls can be deconstructed.

And I use that word *deconstructed* purposefully. As walls are built to serve a particular function, you can't come in trying to tear them down haphazardly, or expecting your husband to take them down just because you need to be let in for the sake of your marriage. You need to take the time to interpret the reason for which the wall came to be, and then it can carefully be dismantled. The atmosphere I'm speaking of, in which this is possible, is a climate where you both can be vulnerable. Where you can open up about yourself without the fear of being put down, judged or treated differently because of what is shared. The tone you want to set in your marriage says to your husband "I am here, and as I promised on the day we wed, I'm not going anywhere. You can be yourself with me. I know you're not perfect, yet I still want to know you on every level, because I love you." **Genesis 2:25** says this: "*And the man and his wife were both naked and were not ashamed.*" This was before sin entered into the world. They had no reason to 'cover up' any part of themselves to hide it from the other. No reason to feel ashamed. Walls down. In marriage, we should be striving to get as close to this as we can.

So, to sum it up... do away with unfruitful talk that sabotages the intimacy between you and your husband! Instead, be *all in* and INVEST in your marriage by creating an atmosphere where trust and vulnerability can thrive, and intimacy can be built.

What are some things you can do to tear down the walls you've built in your relationship?

What passions does your husband have, that you don't have in common, and how can you take an interest in them?

Build Mutual Respect

"Then the Lord God said, "It is not good that the man should be alone; I will make him a helper fit for him.""
— *Genesis 2:18 (ESV)*

The world, today, teaches us total independence of the sexes. A man is looked at as less of a man if he admits his need for his wife, and a woman is viewed as weak if she is thought of as *needing* her husband. There's even a 'battle of the sexes' that has been waging on for centuries. The pendulum swings back and forth. Once, men were regarded as the stronger, more important sex. The husband worked a job for his family, while the wife took care of the home and children by doing all of the cooking and cleaning. Women weren't given their full value, rights or freedoms in this society that esteemed one sex over the other. This caused them to rise up to prove themselves equal. And so now we hear a lot of 'women are better than men because...' or 'a woman can do anything that a man can do, but better,' as well as the downgrading of men. I do have to admit that because of the freedoms and rights women enjoy today, as well as all the advancements in modern technology, men and women are more capable than ever of living without their counterparts. Yet, instead of appreciating our differences, and exploring how we can work in concert with one another, we continue to be in competition to prove the other inferior. This is not the mindset in which God created us. **Genesis 1:26-27** says,

> *"Then God said, "Let us make man in our image,*
> *after our likeness. And let them have dominion over*
> *the fish of the sea and over the birds of the heavens*
> *and over the livestock and over all the earth and*
> *over every creeping thing that creeps on the earth."*
> *So God created man in his own image,*
> *in the image of God he created him;*
> *male and female he created them."* (ESV)

God made *both* men and women in His image, and gave them the mandate to "*have dominion*" together. This sanction is reiterated in the next verse when He talks directly to Adam and Eve:

> *"And God blessed them. And God said to them, "Be fruitful and multiply and fill the earth and subdue it, and have dominion over the fish of the sea and over the birds of the heavens and over every living thing that moves on the earth.""*

God created man, *or mankind,* in His image, but He created mankind as male and female. God created two types of people: male and female, yet He created us all *in His image*. What is all this saying? I believe that God chose not to put all of His image into men only or into women exclusively, but He put certain attributes of His image into men, and other attributes into women, so that when we come together in marriage (particularly and uniquely in marriage, but you can also see glimpses of it in partnerships, at church, in business, in our community, etc.), we can more completely display the image of God to the world together, in our everyday life! And He has commissioned us to *"have dominion"* over the earth and everything on it. But we cannot truly fulfill this commission without one another, and our work to diminish one sex over the other is counterproductive.

What I am trying to say here is that in marriage,

You need your husband and your husband needs you.

For life decisions, *both* of you are needed. For maintaining a home, *both* of you are needed. For raising children, *both* of you are needed. For providing the needs of the household, *both* of you are needed. Don't let the world shame you into denying this to yourself or your husband. He needs to understand where you're at on this. Now, you will function differently. You will assume different roles in everything you aspire to do, but it needs to be done *together*. There's also a hierarchy in which God works to have order, and we do need to operate within it, but husband and wife are equal in importance and standing with Him. And, to have a successful marriage life, coming to terms with this now, instead of later, will help you avoid a lot of headache and heartache in the long run.

In **Genesis 2:18** (at the top), God states that *"It is not good that man should be alone,"* and makes a helper specifically for him. Now this was before sin had entered the world, so when God created Eve, she might have been already perfect for him — — I don't know — — but now we have to work at this thing. We also have to leave room for God to work, which means you have to be a praying wife and led by God. But it helps our view of the type of helper we are when we look at that word *helper* in the Hebrew form. It is the word 'ê-zer (*pronounced ay'-zer*). It means *aid* or *help*. But what is interesting is this is the same word used to describe GOD as a 'helper' in **Psalm 33:20**; **121:1-2**; **124:8**; and in **Hosea 13:9**. Here He calls Himself such! God helps us in ways we cannot help ourselves, so this is obviously not a demeaning or diminutive position. It's a position of strength! It is not like a child who has no understanding of what you are doing, helping you by handing you what you need because they happen to be able to identify the items, but cannot use them to complete the task themselves. No! This is more like the parent that comes alongside a child to help them learn to ride a bike, fix something, bake a cake, or do homework! This helper is someone without whom you cannot do a specific, formidable task. *That's* what a wife is to her husband! It's also like a baseball team, where a coach assigns each player a specific post on the field (pitcher, 1st baseman, 2nd baseman, outfielder, etc.), and if everyone plays their position well, they will most likely succeed. But if an outfielder decides he's better at pitching than the other guy, and takes the mound during the game, the team will be left with no one to catch the fly balls that go to his assigned position, and they will fail miserably! This is the effect a wife can have in her marriage.

But you can only fulfill this when you are working in concert with your husband, *in mutual respect!*

Ecclesiastes 4:9-10 says, *"Two are better than one, because they have a good reward for their toil. For if they fall, one will lift up his fellow. But woe to him who is alone when he falls and has not another to lift him up!"* (ESV)

If you are not treating your husband with respect, he will be worse off than if he were alone, because not only will you not be lifting him up when he falls, but you will also discourage him, and put him down. But, if you treat him with respect and conduct yourself in a manner worthy of respect, you can help him. You can work with him, not against him, and you two will have a good reward for the work you put in together. And if either of you falls, the other will be there to help you up, instead of delivering a swift kick to your downed 'comrade.' Then, neither of you will have to live in fear of falling. You will have each other's back!

Earlier, I mentioned there was a hierarchy that God works in. I was referring to the husband being the head of the wife which is stated in **Ephesians 5:23**. This is one of the ways that God has established order in the marriage relationship. This isn't about who's stronger or who's more fit to lead, as much as it just speaks to His design. God has decided to put the brunt of the responsibility of the marriage relationship on the husband (**Ephesians 5:25-29; I Peter 3:7**). It is the job of the wife, as helpmeet, to help him with this, and her *willful* submission to him is one of the ways that she does this (yes, I used the dreaded 's' word). This means that your attitude in offering your knowledge, opinions and ideas to your husband should display you acknowledge the position that God has given him, and that you will let him lead, whether he does it your way, his way, or some mixture of the two. This starts with you submitting your will and self to God. Ask Him to give you the desire, strength, and wisdom to do this. He is faithful to do it, according to these scriptures:

"...because God is always at work in you to make you willing and able to obey his own purpose."
– Philippians 2:13 GNT

"Whatever you ask in my name, this I will do, that the Father may be glorified in the Son. If you ask me anything in my name, I will do it."
— John 14:13-14 ESV

God has chosen the man to lead in the household, but this doesn't mean he is without many flaws. When someone else is at the helm, it's always easier to pick apart their leadership, and be critical of their shortcomings. Don't get distracted by this with your husband. Instead, work with him and not against him, because if you work against him, you work against your own household. There's a beauty to this that you will only see when it is in motion. It's like a beautiful ballroom dance. God created marriage, and it is good! Like everything else that He creates, it is beautiful, multifaceted and functional.

I'd like to challenge you to give this an honest try. Give yourself the chance to see the beauty of God's design as you live and work with your husband in mutual respect. The more you let go of the indoctrination of this world, and as if slipping into a beautiful couture ballgown, you embrace God's way, the lighter you'll feel. It will be as if you can literally sense the chains falling from your wrists, ankles and neck. There is relief and comfort, joy and peace! This feeling reminds me of the familiar invitation Jesus gives, with promise:

"Come to me, all you who are weary and burdened, and I will give you rest. Take my yoke upon you and learn from me, for I am gentle and humble in heart, and you will find rest for your souls. For my yoke is easy and my burden is light."

— Matthew 11:28-30 (NIV)

In what ways can you improve on showing respect to your husband?

How can you more effectively work in concert with him?

Build Open, Effective Communication

"You shall not hate your brother in your heart, but you shall reason frankly with your neighbor, lest you incur sin because of him. You shall not take vengeance or bear a grudge against the sons of your own people, but you shall love your neighbor as yourself: I am the Lord."
– Leviticus 19:17-18, ESV

Initially, and throughout most of our marriage, Anthony has been very attentive. He's been sensitive to what I needed, and a lot of times *how* I was feeling. He seems to really understand me. On top of that, he's a wonderful gift giver! Fast forward years into our marriage, and my obliging, conscientious husband has fallen off! Things I once could depend on him to do, he no longer did. While he still buys me gifts impulsively, he started missing all the special occasions he had formerly made extra special! Our anniversary, my birthday and Mother's Day are literally within two weeks of each other, and that would just be three big misses in a row, with not much else to look forward to until Christmas. It started with his discontinuing his purchases of stuffed animals for me on every Valentine's and Sweetest Day, which I understood. I had accumulated quite the menagerie, with nowhere to put them all. This was replaced by roses and chocolate-covered fruit traditions, before it seemed like the ritual was abandoned, altogether. My feelings were hurt. I didn't want to say anything, because part of the joy in this was that it was his idea. I felt that he should've known without my having to say anything. I mean, he knew enough to create this tradition of surprises (which I love), and carefully thought-out gifts, so why would he stop… unless he was falling out of love with me! And it went on from there. Me with my hurt feelings, trying to figure out why he stopped doing something that I very much appreciated, stewing over it, instead of just having a conversation with him about it. Maybe you've been there yourself: Frustrated with your husband over something he is or isn't doing, and expressing yourself with your attitude more than your conversation. Maybe your predicament is more serious than mine. Perhaps, you've already told him about it, and you don't feel like you should have to say it again. To you — to myself — I'm saying use *your words*.

Communication in marriage is extremely important, and not just when there's a conflict. Without it, we wouldn't know how our spouse feels about us or how to treat, or not to treat, one another. We would be clueless about our mate's likes and dislikes, what they think and feel about a myriad of subjects, or even how they're doing today. You need to regularly and consistently dialogue with your husband. Let him know what's going on with you; how you're doing and feeling about what's going on in life. Also, be willing to listen to your husband on these things, as well. Try asking about his day, or what's going on with him before unloading on him. I say this as a rule of thumb, not set in stone or regardless of circumstances. If he's not very verbal, pay attention to his countenance and demeanor. They can give hints about what's going on with him, that you can follow up on.

Though no one can explain their entire inner workings, nor can one truly and fully know another, when you incorporate regular verbal correspondence into the rhythms of your life — aside from conversations about the business of the household or the kids — as you evolve, grow, and mature over the years, you can better keep up with each other, and know one another more completely and intimately.

There are many layers to communication, and in marriage we use them all:

- Sharing highlights/lowlights about your day
- Informing your husband on things he needs to know, or choices you have to make together.

- Revealing your inner self to your spouse: what you think about certain things; why you are how you are, or do things how you do them; sharing from your background (growing up, and other life experiences before you met); idiosyncrasies; etc.
- Discussing areas where your marriage is doing well, and where it needs work or attention, from your point of view
- Talking about what you think or feel on any matter
- Addressing offense/Broaching conflict
- Facial expressions
- What you do – you're saying something with your actions; they should back up what you say

This is the reason I say that communication is to be built. There's so much to it, so many layers, that it's not just going to come together on its own without frequency and conscious effort. The first six items describe types of verbal communication. The last two don't, and this is where things can get tricky!

Communicating During Conflict

You may not have a whole lot of control over your facial expressions letting on to your emotions, so you should use words to convey what you're feeling — particularly when you're in conflict. This will at least give context to your sour face, but more importantly, it will give you an opportunity to talk it out and come to some common ground.

Your actions, which are said to speak louder than words, need to be deliberately loving. What you do can speak more boldly — even harsher — than you would if you would just share what's actually going on with you. If you're sad, your actions may convey that you don't want to be bothered. If you're angry, your actions might look more like you've had enough of your spouse. And if your husband is satisfied taking his cues on how you're feeling from your actions, instead of coming right out and asking you, then neither of you are communicating with the other well, resulting in misunderstanding and distance. Those walls I talked about tearing down, go up.

The verse at the beginning of this section (Leviticus 19:17-18) tells us not to harbor ill feelings against our neighbor (a person living nearby), but instead to *reason* with them. It says that we should love them in the way we love ourselves, instead of holding a grudge against them, so we aren't guilty of wrongdoing. As I examine this verse myself, I am being convicted about the situation I described initially.

I have started the conversation about this issue with my husband, but there hasn't been resolution as of yet. As I am writing this, I realize that I have held a grudge against him when I wasn't talking to him about it. I am still tempted to do that, as the situation has not been remedied. I am sharing this with you to reassure you that though I have learned a lot during my marriage, I have yet to master anything. I still have to stay vigilant over many situations, according to what I know, to prevent slipping back into old habits.

Don't Be Completely Uninhibited With Your Words

During confrontation, some things are better left *unsaid*. Your words can injure, causing damage to the marriage relationship, so you want to be careful of what you let fly out of your mouth during an argument. Nagging wears a person down. Do not use words that cut, just to provide yourself with some temporary relief from frustration or anger, or for vengeance. Let's look at what the Bible says about this:

"A fool gives full vent to his spirit, but a wise man quietly holds it back."
— (Proverbs 29:11, ESV)

"When words are many, transgression is not lacking, but whoever restrains his lips is prudent."
— (Proverbs 10:19, ESV)

Also, in confrontation, there's going to be a lot you *want* to say, but let me caution you to keep your words only to what is helpful to convey your point and for resolution. All those other words just muddy the waters of whatever you're trying to say, making it difficult for your husband to be receptive of it or even to perceive it. They also make it more likely that you'll say something hurtful. **Ephesians 4:29** says, *"Do not let any unwholesome talk come out of your mouths, but only what is helpful for building others up according to their needs, that it may benefit those who listen." (NIV)* Use your words to build your husband up, not tear him down.

Proverbs 27:15 – *"A quarrelsome wife is like the dripping of a leaky roof in a rainstorm;" (NIV)*

I wince at this one! If you have water dripping in your house through your roof when it rains, you know you have a problem on your hands! And if the problem doesn't get resolved, it will cause more issues. That water doesn't just drip inside your house, and find its way right on out. It lingers. It builds, and it affects other things. It stains your walls, making them ugly. It waterlogs your furniture, so you can't sit on it anymore. It wreaks havoc on your electronics, rendering them useless. Metal will rust. Fabrics will mold. Wooden furnishings will warp and fall apart. All your stuff will eventually be destroyed, and your home will have an unpleasant stench! It is similar when you continue to complain or pick fights about the same stuff, repeatedly. You will wear him down until he no longer sees the purpose of trying with you. This is what drives many husbands to abdicate their position as head of household, or becoming "uh-huh" husbands (giving verbal agreement, but going about things their own way without a discussion to really consider what you're saying); because at this stage, he just wants you to leave him alone. He will start to dread spending time with you. He won't come to you to share about himself or his experiences to circumvent being criticized over trivial things — or he'll avoid conversation with you altogether. And without openness in your relationship — without you spending time together sharing yourselves — you will not build intimacy and your marriage will erode. **Proverbs 31:10-12** says,

> *"An excellent wife who can find? She is far more precious than jewels. The heart of her husband trusts in her, and he will have no lack of gain. She does him good, and not harm, all the days of her life." (ESV)*

Do not communicate so it is harmful to your husband, and your marriage, strive to do it in a way that will be good for both.

> **Ephesians 4:15 –** *"Instead, speaking the truth in love, we will grow to become in every respect the mature body of him who is the head, that is, Christ." (NIV)*

While some things are better left unsaid, there will be times when you must offer some critique, and when you find yourself in this situation, let it be done *in love.* We don't criticize just to have something negative to say. We hope to bring to light an area in need of improvement, so let your words be sprinkled with love, compassion, kindness, empathy, and patience. Let your comments be constructive. If this is a sticking point for you guys, pray before you get into it. Let God be your help. **Colossians 3:12-14** says,

> *"Put on then, as God's chosen ones, holy and beloved, compassionate hearts, kindness, humility, meekness, and patience, bearing with one another and, if one has a complaint against another, forgiving each other; as the Lord has forgiven you, so you also must forgive. And above all these put on love, which binds everything together in perfect harmony." (ESV)*

Let your words help bring you two together instead of drive a bigger wedge between you.

Don't Fake the Funk!

Stay away from doing the thing where you're upset, he asks you what's wrong, and you say "nothing!" First, you are not being honest in this moment. Second, quietly harping on it in your head does nothing to help the situation. If you need a minute to gather yourself, so you can have a civil conversation, then say that, take a moment, and then talk about it. Saying that you're not upset when you obviously are only adds unnecessary tension to your marriage relationship. Be honest, be real.

So, What Can I Do To Have Healthy Interaction During Conflict?

2 Corinthians 10:3-5 says, *"For though we live in the world, we do not wage war as the world does. The weapons we fight with are not the weapons of the world. On the contrary, they have divine power to demolish strongholds. We demolish arguments and every pretension that sets itself up against the knowledge of God, and we take captive every thought to make it obedient to Christ."*

Notice how this verse mentions that *"though we live in the world, we do not wage war as the world does."* I want you to consider your normal way of handling an argument with your husband and ask yourself, "What about this is too much like the world, and not enough like Christ?" Does it display any of the Fruit of the Spirit: love, joy, peace, faithfulness, goodness, kindness, gentleness, patience, or self-control (Galatians5:22-32)?

The verse also talks about taking *every thought* captive. This is to avoid acting on something that is against what we stand for in Christ. It's also to avoid saying or doing something that will undermine love or trust in your relationship, which you will later regret and have to ask God's forgiveness for. It will also help you resist behaving in a way that may feel good at the time, which may seem to make sense or appear to be what he deserves, yet would not help to advance the situation.

Before letting words gush out of your mouth in anger, frustration or retribution, filter them through these questions:

1. Does what I have to say bring any clarification to the issue at hand?
2. Can I say this in a kinder way; one that shows understanding and/or empathy for his perspective, while clearly expressing the depth of how I feel?
3. Are my motives in saying this purely to communicate to my husband so that he might hear and understand, or am I mostly lashing out?

The objective isn't so much about who's right and who's wrong. You'll end up having a debate and trying to win, and when only one of you wins, the relationship suffers. Your goal should be to better understand one another and then a peaceful consensus on how to move forward.

Listen for the purpose of understanding your husband.

While he's talking, and you hear something you want to address, you may find yourself on edge, waiting for an opportunity to jump in with a rebuttal, or worse – cutting him off. Pay attention when this happens, because at this point, your husband has lost your undivided attention. Redirect your thoughts back to what your man is saying, and wait until he's finished to respond. You may feel you won't remember what you wanted to say once he's done. The most important thing here is that you hear him. If he feels like you don't care what he has to say, he's not going to hear you, either.

Don't be afraid to be vulnerable!

In the movies, when two sides are battling, and one side wants to end the fighting and have peaceful interaction, or they want to reason with the other side, they put their weapons down in a very obvious way. They usually put their hands up to signify that they don't have weapons and come in peace. This usually inspires the other side to put down their arms as well. Vulnerability encourages vulnerability, and it can change a battleground into a discussion table. It takes only one of you to expose your true emotions and open a peaceful line of communication. Exchanging 'attack' words like "you did..." or "you think..." with words like "when you say or do ________, that makes me feel like ______." This also entails being honest about your shortcomings. With the goal being peace and unity, you can't hold back from admitting your wrongs until your spouse admits theirs. You may find yourself at a stalemate. Using attack words or not being willing to admit wrong or areas where we struggle are things we do to avoid appearing weak. No one likes to be weak. We prefer strength, but our true strength comes from Christ. We need to take on the attitude of Paul in **II Corinthians 12:9-10**, after God told him, *"My grace is sufficient for you, for my power is made perfect in weakness."* Paul's response was, *"Therefore I will boast all the more gladly of my weaknesses, so that the power of Christ may rest upon me. For the sake of Christ, then, I am content with weaknesses, insults, hardships, persecutions, and calamities. For when I am weak, then I am strong."* (ESV) Be vulnerable in your marriage conflicts, so God's power can permeate the heart and bring you guys together!

Forgive!

Forgiveness allows us to get to the bottom of what is going on, instead of getting hung up on things like insults which may represent another topic to be discussed at a later time. **Proverbs 19:11** says that *"A man's discretion makes him slow to anger, And it is his glory to overlook a transgression."*

It is imperative you engage with your spouse frequently, consistently, honestly, and respectfully. You should touch base daily, establish regular date nights (*at least* every two weeks), and plan to get away together for a recharge at least annually. And when you have a disagreement or there's an offense, resolve yourself to showing love to your husband throughout the interaction. You have the rest of your life to really get to know one another on the deepest of levels. Use your time wisely, and productively.

How do you plan to incorporate communication into the rhythms of your life with your husband? Write your plans below.

What is one unhealthy practice you can change today about how you communicate with your husband?

Build Your Prayer Life

"Finally, be strong in the Lord and in his mighty power. Put on the full armor of God, so that you can take your stand against the devil's schemes. For our struggle is not against flesh and blood, but against the rulers, against the authorities, against the powers of this dark world and against the spiritual forces of evil in the heavenly realms. Therefore put on the full armor of God, so that when the day of evil comes, you may be able to stand your ground, and after you have done everything, to stand. Stand firm then, with the belt of truth buckled around your waist, with the breastplate of righteousness in place, and with your feet fitted with the readiness that comes from the gospel of peace. In addition to all this, take up the shield of faith, with which you can extinguish all the flaming arrows of the evil one. Take the helmet of salvation and the sword of the Spirit, which is the word of God.

And pray in the Spirit on all occasions with all kinds of prayers and requests. With this in mind, be alert and always keep on praying for all the Lord's people."
— Ephesians 6:10-18 (NIV)

If there is one thing I have learned over the years about where my effectiveness as a wife and mom truly lies, it would have to be in prayer. I have striven a lot to get people to see things from the right perspective, using logic and even the Word of God. These devices don't always help the situation. Too many times, they only seem to put a bandage on it, in that my advice is taken for the simple purpose of getting me off their back. And when I push too hard, I seem overbearing or controlling. But if you want some *real* change in your marriage — I'm talking about a change down to the heart — I suggest you keep a running conversation with The Lord about *everything*.

Jesus permeated His life with prayer: He started days with prayer (Mark 1:35); He ended arduous days of ministry in prayer (Mark 6:30-46). He prayed a blessing over food before meals (Matthew 14:19; 15:36; 26:26). He prayed vehemently before making a major decision or major events in His life (Luke 6:12-13). He went into the wilderness to fast (which includes prayer) for forty days and nights before He started His earthly ministry (Matthew 4:1-17). On the evening before His arrest, Jesus prayed for His disciples and all who would believe in Him in the future (John 17:1-26). Then, right before they came to arrest

Him, Jesus prayed, and prayed, and PRAYED, until drops [like] blood ran down His head (Luke 22:39-48; Mathew 26:36-46)!

You're gonna pray on things as they come up, but you want to do some of what I call 'preemptive' or 'offensive' prayer, where you're praying over your husband before anything even comes up. Pray over his day, for him in his employment, and for his leadership: for wisdom; discernment; guidance; that it is done in love; etc. Pray for your marriage relationship, and for your sex life. And still, you want to pray for God to help him in the areas in which he struggles, for his hardships, his endeavors, and so on. Pray for yourself: that you work in concert with him, and not against him; that you understand what submission looks like for you, in your marriage; pray for the strength to do all that you know you should do, but struggle with. Pray that God continues to bring you closer together in loving, intimate relationship, and that He helps you both find common ground with one another in all of the areas you are facing. The bottom line here is that you want to invite God into your marriage and seek Him to cover it *daily*.

In Ephesians 6 (above), after telling us that our real enemies are not the people we see in front of us, but that they are actually unseen spiritual forces with an agenda for this world, and that we need spiritual armor provided to us by God to withstand attacks by this enemy, the writer tells us to "...*pray in the Spirit on all occasions with all kinds of prayers and requests.*" This verse tells us to bring *all types* of prayers before The Lord and *all the time*. Prayer is conversing with God. Just like in your relationship with people, sometimes you talk to them because you have a request: a favor to ask, advice, etc. Other times you talk to them because you just need to process or get something off your chest. Still there are times you converse with them to share good or bad news, to share something that you've learned, to thank them for doing something kind, to check in on how they're doing, or just to spend some time with them. There are all types of reasons we converse with each other. It should be no different with God. I have a habit of talking to Him as if He's right there beside me (which He kinda is ☺). It is my inner dialogue. And if you ever catch me 'talking to myself,' He is usually the One I am actually talking to. It's just a regular dialogue like I would have with anyone else I was hanging out with all day. This is my way of living out the '*pray without ceasing*' command in I Thessalonians 5:17. Yours may look differently, but we should all be keeping up with our relationship with God. Not in the way we may be "Keeping Up With The Kardashians," where you check in with them at the regularly scheduled time of once a week, to watch a carefully curated broadcast of events from their lives, according to how some producer wants to shape your feelings or response. God wants your true reality, with all of the boring bits and your struggles, and He wants to hear about your joy and what you're thankful for too!

I like how other versions of this verse say 'supplication' instead of 'requests.' I like that word better because of what it means: *the action of asking or begging for something earnestly or humbly*. The two adverbs in the definition of supplication speak to the perspective and faith you must have as you approach God in prayer. *Humbly,* because you have to understand that though you may have an idea of how you think the best way to address the situation is, you also know that you can't see or wholly comprehend the full extent of the effect that any given solution may have, yet you know that God does. And you've got to come *earnestly,* because you have to sincerely believe that God hears you, He cares about what is going on, and that He is the only One with the power to affect the situation with the most complete, best possible outcome. Then, and only then, have you fully put yourself in His capable hands! **Hebrews 11:6** says, *"And without faith it is impossible to please God, because anyone who comes to him must believe that he exists and that he rewards those who earnestly seek him." (NIV)*

Back to the verse in Ephesians, which says, *"...With this in mind, be alert and always keep on praying for all the Lord's people."* The *"with this in mind..."* points back to where it was talking about how *"we do not wrestle against flesh and blood..."*. We have to continually keep this at the forefront of our minds, and use our spiritual weapon of prayer when we're wrestling through something in our marriage. The adversary will have you looking at your husband as if *he* is the enemy. Don't be fooled: your husband is not your enemy. Sometimes he may be influenced by the enemy or blinded to what is right, or maybe he has yet to find the strength or conviction to do what he already knows is right in his head — but he is ultimately on your side. When you see that your husband is not doing right, take it to The Lord in prayer! If you discover an area where you are spiritually strong, but he is spiritually underdeveloped, bring it before The Lord! If you observe your husband wrestling over whether — or even *how* — to trust God on a matter, seek The Lord on his behalf! And while you're at it, talk to God about the best way for you to respond. **I Peter 5:7** says, *"Cast all your anxiety on him because he cares for you." (NIV)* As you strive with your husband to feel your way through a tough decision, try to convince him you need to change up how you do something, or whatever your challenge may be, you need to bring the matter before God! You can do that together (which is best), or on your own (which is still really good). **Philippians 4:6-7** says this:

> *"Do not be anxious about anything, but in every situation, by prayer and petition, with thanksgiving, present your requests to God. And the peace of God, which transcends all understanding, will guard your hearts and your minds in Christ Jesus." (NIV)*

I don't know about you, but when I'm going back and forth with my husband over an issue that I'm passionate about, and is stressing me out, I have trouble speaking to him without my anxiety oozing out all over the conversation. This can look like me raising my voice, cutting him off, or sometimes lashing out. At this moment patience, kindness and gentleness are far down on my list of importance. I have no peace! Yet, there's something about when you honestly and resolutely bring your requests, concerns, or problems to The Lord. You get peace about the situation. The more you do this, the more you learn to trust Him, the more earnest you'll be in bringing your concerns to Him and leaving them with Him! Too often, I have wasted precious time trying to get my husband to see things from my perspective, when all the while I should have been pursuing The Lord to open his eyes, give him strength, give him wisdom, give him whatever he needed. I have learned not to get too worked up when I can't seem to get through to him because I know that I can always get through to God! God has a plan for your marriage! His work will be done in perfect timing, and nothing can stop Him from doing what He's gonna do!

"Be joyful in hope, patient in affliction, faithful in prayer."

— Romans 12:12 (NIV)

On what issues have you been striving with your husband — or even trying to control — where you just need to give it over to The Lord and let Him work it out?

How can you pray for your husband today?

Work On Yourself

"Why do you see the speck that is in your brother's eye, but do not notice the log that is in your own eye? Or how can you say to your brother, 'Let me take the speck out of your eye,' when there is the log in your own eye? You hypocrite, first take the log out of your own eye, and then you will see clearly to take the speck out of your brother's eye."
— Matthew 7:3-5 ESV

Okay, so by the verse above, you probably already know where I'm going with this... We, as human beings, have an innate ability to look at someone other than ourselves and point out all their faults, while looking at ourselves through rose-colored glasses. We view others in the light of their shortcomings, and what they do, compared to what we think they should do, while evaluating ourselves on our best qualities and our 'good intentions' that may not even be evident in what we do.

This perspective on ourselves versus others can stunt our own growth and make us critics of others, devaluing and discouraging them. The temptation for this is great in marriage.

When you're married, it's easy to pick your husband apart, pointing out what he does wrong, or how he may be falling short, but you must resist this habit. Let's examine this very familiar passage in 1 Corinthians:

> *"Love is patient and kind; love does not envy or boast; it is not arrogant or rude. It does not insist on its own way; it is not irritable or resentful; it does not rejoice at wrongdoing, but rejoices with the truth. Love bears all things, believes all things, hopes all things, endures all things."*
> ***— 1 Corinthians 13:4-7 ESV***

Notice how it tells us that love is *patient and kind...* as a wife, you have to allow The Lord to do His work in your husband, in His time. I remember becoming impatient with my husband over financial issues. I wanted God to 'fix him' in that area. I was praying that He would. I was so focused on one area where he was falling short, that I had paid no attention — much less acknowledged — the areas where God *had* been working, and changing him for the better. Now that's being unappreciative of what God is doing, as well as for what my husband had been improving upon! Here I was, thinking I knew what needed to change to make our lives better (which was him), and all the while, I had a lack of patience, my lack of patience led me to be disrespectful to my husband, rude at times, and plain old unkind! And to make matters worse, I had the audacity to look at God like "why haven't you fixed him yet? I've been praying..." The Lord came back real quick like, "*Who are you to tell Me in what order I need to work on my son? If you would just look at what I have already done in him, and focus more on your own faults and weaknesses, you wouldn't be so dissatisfied.*" I had problems, but I was focused on his, not even noticing my own. If this doesn't sound familiar to you yet, just wait until you've been married for a while. When all of the infatuation and fuzzy feelings of the courting stage wears off, you will see your husband as he is: a flawed individual. Then after a while of that, you'll be tempted to think of him or operate as if his flaws are the main ones affecting your marriage and/or family life. Don't fall for the 'okie-doke'.

Looking at the scripture at the beginning of this section, from Matthew 7, I want you to note the similarity between me in the situation I described above, and that the person who is trying to help the other with the speck in their eye, but has a *log* in their own eye. Here I was, nagging my husband about doing better with the money. We weren't homeless, or even without our own vehicle. We had very little income, which meant that to stay afloat, one had to be very precise about handling the funds. Any misstep could cause the dropping of a proverbial ball. I was being pushy,

I nagged, I attempted unsuccessfully to do it better – all because I was impatient, and respecting my husband was low on my list of what I thought would be helpful in our marriage and building our life together. I was blinded by my impatience, and insecurity of what others might think if we weren't able to keep up or keep things together (i.e., the log in my eye).

Make sure you are removing logs (and specks, even) from your own eye. Ask God to point out areas where you're falling short and give you the knowledge, will, and strength to straighten up. You will find there is always *something* you can be focusing on within yourself. It will keep you busy from focusing too much on your husband's shortcomings, and all the while The Lord will be molding you into a beautiful, godly wife, mother, woman... help meet!

What are some ways you can show more love to your husband? Write them below, talk to God about them. Ask for His forgiveness and help, and jot down some ways you can improve.

Ask God to help you identify two areas you can improve in as a wife, mother, daughter, sister, etc. Ask Him to show you how you can better serve and interact with your family members.

It's Not All About You

Then God said, "Let us make mankind in our image,
in our likeness, so that they may rule over the fish
in the sea and the birds in the sky, over the livestock
and all the wild animals, and over all the creatures
that move along the ground."
So God created mankind in his own image,
in the image of God he created him;
male and female he created them.
— ***Genesis 1:26-27***

In this world, we are taught that marriage is about us. We see it all the time in the movies: people coming together because they make each other happy; people coming together because they share romantic feelings for one another; people that decide to be together because one of them feels so deeply for the other that 'they can't bear to live another minute without them in their lives'; people that get together because they realize that they have so much in common; people who end up getting together because they realize that one person has something that inspires them to become a better person, or complete them in some kind of way; and so on. There's nothing really wrong with any of these things, and these are certainly some of the reasons that we end up with our spouse. It's just that a lasting marriage needs a purpose that goes beyond personal needs, desires or feelings, because these things are forever changing.

Now, when we look to the Creator of the marital union, we see a different reason for marriage. In **Ephesians 5:31-32**, Paul writes this: *""Therefore a man shall leave his father and mother and hold fast to his wife, and the two shall become one flesh." This mystery is profound, and I am saying that it refers to Christ and the church," (ESV).* As he is speaking of the man 'holding fast' to his wife, and becoming one flesh with her, he calls it a mystery, and that it '*refers to Christ and the church.*' Here, Paul says that when a man and woman come together in holy matrimony, they become one — not two — flesh (**Matthew 19:4-6**), never to be separated, and this joining of the man and woman references Christ and the church. Meaning that the marriage relationship should demonstrate, or resemble, the relationship between Christ and His church. Therein lies the real purpose for marriage.

If we back it up to when Paul describes the roles of the man and his wife within the marriage, we see a direct correlation to our duties as it relates to the relationship between Christ and the church:

"Wives, submit to your own husbands, as to the Lord. For the husband is the head of the wife even as Christ is the head of the church, his body, and is himself its Savior. Now as the church submits to Christ, so also wives should submit in everything to their husbands. Husbands, love your wives, as Christ loved the church and gave himself up for her, that he might sanctify her, having cleansed her by the washing of water with the word, so that he might present the church to himself in splendor, without spot or wrinkle or any such thing, that she might be holy and without blemish."

— Ephesians 5:22-27 ESV

Here, wives are told to submit to their own husbands, but notice the description of *how* we are supposed to do this: "*...as to the Lord*." We make our own decision to submit to The Lord. We don't do it out of compulsion. We do it from the freedom we have to choose. We do it because we love Him, and we trust Him. We may not be perfect at it, but we are continually striving to be better at it, as we are coming to a clearer understanding of what it looks like in our individual lives. It is the same with our husbands. Though, the clear line of difference is as we discussed in the previous section: that God is perfect, and our husbands are not. Yet even though we know that God is perfect, what I find common in this is that we don't always understand or agree with what He — or our husband — does. In God's case, this is because He is an infinitely greater being than us, according to **Isaiah 55:8-9**: *"For my thoughts are not your thoughts, neither are your ways my ways," declares the Lord. "As the heavens are higher than the earth, so are my ways higher than your ways and my thoughts than your thoughts." (NIV)*

Back to the passage in Ephesians, it explains that the husband is to love his wife as Christ loved the Church, even bringing up Christ's willingness to give Himself up in place of His Church. I do want to point out the passage on submission also gets twisted and misused. Some husbands use it to control their wives, keeping them in a place of insignificance and/or bondage to him. But, since Paul says, *"as to the Lord,"* we have to look at how we are to submit to the Lord: and that is willingly. Jesus doesn't force anyone to submit to Him. He only *invites* us to do so, letting us know there are many *benefits* to accepting His love gift:

"Come to me, all who labor and are heavy laden, and I will give you rest. Take my yoke upon you, and learn from me, for I am gentle and lowly in heart, and you will find rest for your souls. For my yoke is easy, and my burden is light."
— Matthew 11:28-30 (ESV)

"Humble yourselves, therefore, under the mighty hand of God so that at the proper time he may exalt you,"
— I Peter 5:6 (ESV)

"See what great love the Father has lavished on us, that we should be called children of God! And that is what we are..."
— 1 John 3:1 (NIV)

In addition, we do not have to submit to our husbands completely quietly, where we aren't to share our own concerns, and ideas. We are actually encouraged to do this with The Lord in **Philippians 4:6**, *"do not be anxious about anything, but in everything by prayer and supplication with thanksgiving let your requests be made known to God," (ESV).* God wants us to share our requests with him. Now, He doesn't guarantee that we will receive all that we ask for, but He definitely encourages us to share with Him. And in **1 Peter 5:7** it says, *"casting all your anxieties on him, because he cares for you," (ESV)* shows us that the Lord wants to hear about our concerns, and He cares about what concerns us. We should be able to expect our husbands to listen to our thoughts on decisions that have to be made, as well as what may trouble us about these decisions or otherwise.

This brings me to the part where Paul tells husbands to love their wives, but specifically *"...as Christ loved the church and gave himself up for her..."* This points to a sacrificial love. Jesus was meek, and humbled Himself to come down here and live a tough life, ultimately giving it up as a sacrifice to repair our relationship with God, make a way for us to be forgiven and cleansed of our sins, so we can be free to live for God on this earth, and to live with Him when we depart it.

"In your relationships with one another, have the same mindset as Christ Jesus: Who, being in very nature God, did not consider equality with God something to be used to his own advantage; rather, he made himself nothing by taking the very nature of a servant, being made in human likeness. And being found in appearance as a man, he humbled himself by becoming obedient to death— even death on a cross!"

— Philippians 2:5-8 (NASB)

"For God so loved the world that he gave his one and only Son, that whoever believes in him shall not perish but have eternal life."

— John 3:16 (NIV)

Through marriage, God has blessed us with the task and opportunity of painting this picture of the greatness of His love relationship with the Church to the world! As we walk out this beautiful illustration, we get to experience it in a very tangible way! If we can but only remember that the purpose of marriage isn't for our own glory, and enjoyment, but God's, even though The Lord does grant us fulfillment and joy in the process. When we are submitted to His will, there are great things The Lord can accomplish through us! Do you want to be found amongst the faithful?

"For the eyes of the Lord run to and fro throughout the whole earth, to show Himself strong on behalf of those whose heart is loyal to Him."

— 2 Chronicles 16:9 (ESV)

Pray and ask God to reveal attitudes and behaviors you may have that hinder God's plan of using your marriage to tell His love story of redemption to the world. Confess them and write them down here.

Ask for His help in getting on the right path to submitting to Him in this. Sit quietly and wait for Him to answer. Write down what He tells you.

Your Body Is Not Your Own

"But because of the temptation to sexual immorality, each man should have his own wife and each woman her own husband. The husband should give to his wife her conjugal rights, and likewise the wife to her husband. For the wife does not have authority over her own body, but the husband does. Likewise the husband does not have authority over his own body, but the wife does. Do not deprive one another, except perhaps by agreement for a limited time, that you may devote yourselves to prayer; but then come together again, so that Satan may not tempt you because of your lack of self-control."

— I Corinthians 7:2-5 (ESV)

First off, TV and the media portrays marriage as the place where sex goes to die. They paint this picture that all kinds of fun, and exciting sex is happening with single people, but once you get married, it all comes to a screeching halt. They act like in marriage you just have sex in the missionary position, and that it's more so an act of duty. This couldn't be further from the truth. Within marriage, you can have the most fulfilling sex life, because marriage is the container in which God created sex to be enjoyed! In this unique relationship, we get to know one another in our triumphs and failures. We get to see each other in ways and situations that no one else gets to know them in. We get to know, love and care for each other in the most intimate ways. We get to support each other through many circumstances in life. We get to relate to one another in ways that no one else would ever understand us! And we take all of this knowledge, love and intimacy with us into the bedroom, and it is BEAUTIFUL! We don't get bored having sex with the same person, year after year. Instead, we build on what we know about each other sexually, sometimes still finding new ways to please one another, all the while being challenged to continue to get to know an ever-evolving person, blossoming year after year! We go from student to expert in pleasing our spouse, and then back to student in some areas.

The world will tell you that your body is your own, and that you can do with it as you please, but the Bible teaches two things about the ownership of the body of a believer: First, that it is the temple (or dwelling place) of the Holy Spirit. We were purchased by the blood of Christ, and that we are to honor God with our bodies (read **I Corinthians 6:19-20**); and second, if we are married, it teaches us that our bodies belong to our spouse (referenced above). The first one applies to all believers, and is why we are to reserve sex to be enjoyed within the confines of marriage. The second is speaking to married couples specifically. In marriage, both rules apply. Paul qualifies God's ownership of our bodies by reminding us that Jesus paid for our redemption by the shedding of His own blood. We all once belonged to Satan, because of sin in the world, but Jesus paid for us to be able to become His again. And for us who have accepted that gift, we must be obedient to the One who saved us.

I want to encourage you to not turn your husband down in the bedroom simply because you 'don't feel like it', or you're 'not in the mood.' The scripture above talks about avoiding temptation, and the lack of bedroom activity certainly can make a spouse more susceptible to temptation. But it is not the only cause or cure for it. People commit adultery for many reasons, so it is best that each spouse work on themselves inwardly, as well as on their *entire* marriage, to keep oneself and help one another not fall victim to temptation. But if you neglect coming together in the 'marriage bed,' then you may be leaving your husband vulnerable to all the sexual temptation available to him out in this world. Sexual intimacy is a *need* that God gave us all, to be fulfilled only within marriage. So, you are the only one that can legitimately fill this need for your husband. To deprive him of it simply because you 'are not in the mood tonight' is unkind, to say the least.

Also, as couples engage in sex with one another, they are being bound in oneness physically, spiritually and emotionally. **I Corinthians 6:16** says, *"Do you not know that he who unites himself with a prostitute is one with her in body? For it is said, "The two will become one flesh,"" (NIV).* Within the confines of marriage, being bound like this is a good thing! It helps to build a deeper relationship together. It is one way God takes the two and makes them one. This is supported by science because we know that oxytocin, dubbed as the 'love hormone,' intensifies our bonding experience with one another. Oxytocin levels are increased when we hug, kiss, or have sex. It also affects our empathy, trust, group memories, and other areas that undergird a person-to-person relationship.

Last, people say things like "God only made sex for procreation." Well, if we read the Bible, we see this is only *partially* true. In Genesis 1:28, after making the man and woman, God does tell them to be fruitful and multiply. And we all know that the only way to do this physically is to have sex, get pregnant and have babies. But then consider **Proverbs 5:18 & 19**:

> *"May your fountain be blessed, and may you rejoice in the wife of your youth. A loving doe, a graceful deer — may her breasts satisfy you always, may you ever be intoxicated with her love." (NIV)*

With language like *"may her breasts satisfy you always"* and *"may you ever be intoxicated with her love,"* this is apparently not talk of procreation, but more like recreation! You can't expect a husband to always be satisfied by his wife's breasts, or intoxicated with her love without experiencing said breasts and 'lovin' on the regular. God gave sex as a gift to married couples. It is an activity for us to enjoy. We keep it between ourselves, and share in it with one another privately as our own sexy little secret. *God wants to bless this*! So enjoy! ;-)

Pray and ask God to bless your sexual relationship. When you feel that your desire for sex is diminishing, pray, then have a conversation with your husband about it, and see if the two of you can come together on ways to combat this. Write down some things you come up with here.

Maybe there are some things you can do to help keep yourself 'into it.' Write some ideas down here.

Have Beauty On Lock

"Wives, in the same way submit yourselves to your own husbands so that, if any of them do not believe the word, they may be won over without words by the behavior of their wives, when they see the purity and reverence of your lives. Your beauty should not come from outward adornment, such as elaborate hairstyles and the wearing of gold jewelry or fine clothes. Rather, it should be that of your inner self, the unfading beauty of a gentle and quiet spirit, which is of great worth in God's sight. For this is the way the holy women of the past who put their hope in God used to adorn themselves."

— I Peter 3:1-5a NIV

You ever meet someone and find them attractive? Then you get to know them better, and their personality is so undesirable it affects the way you view them, to where you don't even see them as attractive anymore?

They may even cause your upper lip to curl in disgust. This is basically the lesson I want to get across to you today.

When Anthony and I were dating, in addition to the deeper connections we had, he was very attracted to me physically. He also found me funny and charming (cute). I knew all this, and I leveraged it to my advantage. These attributes are nice to have, but I learned pretty quickly not to get too caught up in these things, in regards to my marriage. I needed to put a greater focus on my more meaningful qualities. Background, ethnicity, physical features, etc., are things you cannot help. Never get too distracted trying to play these up — particularly in your marriage relationship.

You're going to be with this man for the rest of his or your life. Your face is in danger of becoming common to him. And I can tell you from experience that your physical attributes will diminish, day by day, year by year, decade by decade — no matter how hard you work, and someone prettier, funnier or more charming can always be found. You need something deeper to reinforce that beauty on the outside. You're going to need a lot more substance to continue to be the prize of his life. I'm not saying you don't have substance now. Every woman has varying portions of intelligence, fun, humor, adventure, knowledge, compassion, etc. These are great qualities, which definitely add to your outer beauty, but since God is the Creator of marriage, we must look to Him to more precisely understand how it works. In **1 Peter 3:3-4**, wives are told

> *"Do not let your adornment be merely outward— arranging the hair, wearing gold, or putting on fine apparel— rather let it be the hidden person of the heart, with the incorruptible beauty of a gentle and quiet spirit, which is very precious in the sight of God." (NKJV)*

The first part of that *"Do not let your adornment be merely outward arranging the hair, wearing gold, or putting on fine apparel..."* tells us not to let our beauty be the only thing people see on the outside. I love how the writer prefaces what's coming up next with this statement. He does not dismiss outward beauty as something not to bother with. And he tells us exactly what he's talking about: hair styles, jewelry and fine clothing. He doesn't say "Don't do these things," or "This is not at all where your beauty comes from," but he's careful to say, "Don't let it stop there," or "That's not all you have to work with." He says, *"...rather let it be the hidden person of the heart, with the incorruptible beauty of a gentle and quiet spirit, which is very precious in the sight of God."* He's telling us to get ourselves together underneath the skin! He's giving us beauty secrets that don't fade, wear off or become common place: a gentle and quiet spirit! **Proverbs 31:30** says, *"Charm is deceitful and beauty is passing, But a woman who fears the LORD, she shall be praised." (NKJV)* Peter just clued us in on some of what it looks like to be a woman who fears The Lord! He's helping us understand what *lasting beauty* is!

During the pandemic of COVID-19, and all the video meetings we've had, I really got an understanding of how light affects how you can look, as well as the importance of having good, direct light shining on you. Bad lighting can make even the most beautiful of women look less than desirable. Depending on where the shadows fall, she can look haggard, like she has bags under her eyes and hasn't slept in forever! Her skin can look very dull, textured and unappealing. But more favorable lighting, and the right angles, can make the same woman look glorious! It can showcase a smooth, glowing complexion, or put her best side on display! Now we're seeing her in a new light! This is what a gentle and quiet spirit can do for us in our marriages. Every time you exhibit these behaviors, your husband can view you in a more *favorable* light! What he is seeing and experiencing in you is captivating to him. It's new. Every time you conduct yourself in this manner, the circumstances are different. It's like a fresh experience! Your husband gets to view you in a new light!

These character traits of a gentle and quiet spirit have become more rarely displayed in our society today, so you can't expect a lot of encouragement from non-Bible believers, and even amongst some who do believe, in this area. People have the misconception that having this demeanor is equal to being a doormat, or weak. We're taught to raise all kinds of heck to get our way or to get our point across. If someone shouts at you, you shout back, and louder! Well, God tells us in **Proverbs 15:1** that *"A soft answer turns away wrath, but a harsh word stirs up anger." (NKJV)* A good rule of thumb in marriage is 'Don't be too concerned about thc opinions of others,' especially when they conflict with what God's Word has to say. Stick to pleasing God, and taking care of your husband. And if your husband is falling short, don't abandon being obedient to God to set him straight. Be respectful about engaging him this way, or just leave it to The Lord. The Bible tells us in **1 Corinthians 10:31** *"So, whether you eat or drink, or whatever you do, do all to the glory of God," (ESV)* and then there's **Romans 12:19** - *"Beloved, never avenge yourselves, but leave it to the wrath of God, for it is written, "Vengeance is mine, I will repay, says the Lord."" (ESV)* And so we must always keep these things in mind. Not to say you can never disagree with your husband, or talk to him about areas where he is struggling, or not doing well, or not doing right. Just approach these things with him prayerfully, with respect and love. Never from a place of condescension, forcefulness or attack. And if he doesn't take heed, bring it to your Heavenly Father.

Peter wraps up this statement by informing us that this type of beauty is *"very precious in the sight of God."* Man may or may not understand the value of this kind of beauty in your marriage, but The Lord *greatly values* it! And His opinion isn't based on how anyone presents themselves on the outside, but on the truth of who you really are! **1 Samuel**

16:7b says *"...For the Lord sees not as man sees: man looks on the outward appearance, but the Lord looks on the heart." (ESV)* Practice having a gentle and quiet spirit. Seek the Lord on what that looks like in your marriage life. He will show you! The Apostle John writes to those who believe in the Name of the Son of God (Jesus), in **1 John 5:14-15**,

> *"And this is the confidence that we have toward him, that if we ask anything according to his will he hears us. And if we know that he hears us in whatever we ask, we know that we have the requests that we have asked of him." (ESV)*

The key words here are *'according to His will.'* Obviously, if our God cherishes the beauty of a gentle and quiet spirit, then when you earnestly ask Him to help you with this, you can be *assured* that He will oblige you! Isn't that awesome?! Doesn't that fact take some of the weight off your shoulders? Anytime you seek God to help you do the things He has commanded or ordained you to do, you can be *sure* that He will do it! So, YES, strive for this! But in your striving, seek The Lord!

Now, let us not completely abandon the outward appearance. The scripture from 1 Samuel, above, does state that man indeed looks on the outward appearance. And you did marry a man for sure! He will definitely appreciate that gentle and quiet spirit, but do *accent* it with styling your hair beautifully, dressing nicely, and accessorizing yourself. Not to say you have to carry the pressure of having this together all the time. Just make sure that it's not neglected. As they say, the best man is still just a man at best! 😉

Pray about this today. As The Lord reveals, write down some ways you can display that gentle and quiet spirit in your marriage.

Let Joy Thrive In Your Heart

"...Do not be grieved, for the joy of the Lord is your strength."
– Nehemiah 8:10b (NASB)

"Consider it all joy, my brethren, when you encounter various trials, knowing that the testing of your faith produces endurance. And let endurance have its perfect result, so that you may be perfect and complete, lacking in nothing."
– James 1:2-4 (NASB)

If I asked you what the atmosphere in your home was like, what would you say? Would you be able to say it is sunny and joy-filled, or would you report that it's cloudy with a chance of rain? Is it like a pour down complete with dark clouds, lightning and thunder, or is it stiflingly oppressive with desert-like temperatures and no relief from precipitation in sight? In a lot of ways, we as wives can set the climate for our home. It can be our choice. We can choose the *perspective* we're going to live in, whether we choose to harp on the negative, or rest our minds on the positive — not ignoring what's wrong, but giving it to The Lord, and looking to Him to create opportunities for you to be an example or speak on it, or for Him to take care of what's going on in a family member's heart, all while thanking Him for what is good.

What we allow our minds to meditate on manifests in our attitude. Like, if we focus our attention on what we have — a roof over our head, food, transportation, items of comfort, a husband and/or children that return our affections, or display good attributes of character, etc. — we *feel* more grateful and content. When a wife is content, she feels happier and can more easily show appreciation for those who contribute to her contentment, like her husband for instance. This inspires her husband, helping him feel like what he has done — or is doing — is well received, and encouraging him to continue or maybe even do more or better. Whereas, when we concentrate on what we don't have, we feel more like we're lacking, and we become discontent. When a wife is discontent, she generally feels disheartened in mood and spirit, and finds it harder to show gratefulness or appreciation — specifically to her husband. This lack of gratefulness in her attitude and actions can be interpreted by him as what he has done, or is doing, isn't good enough or effective, and that can make him feel like no matter what he does, he can never please her — so why even try?

Philippians 4:4-8 *says: "Rejoice in the Lord always. I will say it again: Rejoice! Let your gentleness be evident to all. The Lord is near. Do not be anxious about anything, but in every situation, by prayer and petition, with thanksgiving, present your requests to God. And the peace of God, which transcends all understanding, will guard your hearts and your minds in Christ Jesus. Finally, brothers and sisters, whatever is true, whatever is noble, whatever is right, whatever is pure, whatever is lovely, whatever is admirable—if anything is excellent or praiseworthy—think about such things." (NIV)*

Here, we are being challenged to always find a reason to rejoice, and to *"let our gentleness be evident to all."* Joy is contagious! When people observe you with a joyful demeanor, they are more likely to feel a little joy themselves. Smiles are infectious! When we're around someone that smiles, we usually smile too! Barring something terrible happening in someone's life, they just can't help it!

The passage doesn't want you to just 'put on a brave face' or paint on a smile. It tells us *how* we can see our way clear to find the joy in our lives. The first thing to do is to bring all of what concerns you to God in prayer, instead of letting it get under your skin and steal your joy. We talked about the importance of prayer in your marriage for receiving God's peace in the midst of hard times. This *"peace... which transcends all understanding"* will protect your heart from hardening, and your mind from getting lost in anxiety or despair, so that you don't lose your joy. The second thing we are told to do is to focus on the good things going on around us. Sin in the world causes us to have pain and trials in this life, but that doesn't negate that God is good, and that His goodness is evident in our lives if we look for it. As we remind ourselves of the goodness God has shown us, we maintain our joy, and are better equipped to deal with the hard things of life. **Proverbs 17:22** says that *"A joyful heart is good medicine, but a crushed spirit dries up the bones." (ESV)* Concentrating only, or mostly, on your struggles is not good for you. You need to develop a habit of paying attention to the manifestations of God's grace in your life.

You also want to promote an attitude of gratitude for your husband. One way you can do this is by thanking God for him each day when you pray. And I don't mean "God, thank you for my husband." Be specific. Thank God for certain things about him that are good. This will help you to continue to view him in a positive light, instead of getting stuck on things you don't like about him, or what he's done (or does) that you don't agree with.

Proverbs 4:23 says *"Above all else, guard your heart, for everything you do flows from it." (NIV)* When we allow joy to abide in our heart, it will show in how we conduct ourselves and in what we say and do. But when we allow a broken spirit to dry us up of joy all the way to the bone, that will equally affect what comes out of us. Lovely Daughter of God, you do not want to become the woman described in this verse:

> *"It is better to live in a corner of a roof than in a house shared with a contentious woman."*
> ***—Proverbs 21:9 (NASB)***

It doesn't do your marriage any good to make your husband feel he needs to avoid you to this extent. To be a wife that is always causing him sorrow or grief by the venomous words that spill out of your mouth, or the vexing things you do, can be harmful to the joy in your home as well as to the state of your marriage. This helps nothing; it only hurts. It doesn't move anything forward; it only hinders. Should you find you are already there, I would advise you to stop immediately, seek The Lord in prayer — with fasting if you can — and find what you can appreciate about your husband. Everyone has redeeming qualities. If you can only find one thing, pray thanks to God for that one thing every day, and *tell it to your husband*. You need to admit to him the harm you have caused in the marriage. I realize that he may have caused some too. Pray about this as well, but working on what you can do to improve the state of your marriage can keep you busy enough.

You may find you need to see a counselor. I recommend a faith-based counselor. This can be a pastor or elder at your church, or a therapist. You can see one as a couple, but you may want to see one on your own as well. If your husband will not go with you, getting good counsel yourself can still be very helpful to you and your marriage.

God can and will work wondrous things through the tough situations you go through in your marriage. He is constantly refining you. He's working on you and your husband to be better versions of yourselves, while perfecting your marriage to display a purer love to the world — like that of Christ's love for the Church. If you can weather a storm without adding more difficulty to the situation, or even love one another through it, you will come out on the other end with a closer bond and deeper intimacy.

Do you see all the influence your perspective can have on your relationship with your husband? I know it takes two to have a good marriage, and it can be hard when you feel like "But he keeps doing this..." or "Things can start improving if he would just begin to (fill in the blank)." These can be things that your husband doesn't know and needs to be educated on, or they can be actions that blatantly go against what he knows to be right, but either way they are matters of the heart that only God can fix anyway. This is why the scriptures speak to God's greatness and good character, and how we should put our hope in Him, and not in people, or even in our own understanding of things.

Put your trust in God. Hang on to your joy. The joy will give you strength as you prayerfully seek opportunities to work on advancing your way through marital difficulty.

"But let all who take refuge in you be glad; let them ever sing for joy. Spread your protection over them, that those who love your name may rejoice in you."
— Psalms 5:11(NIV)

"And we know that all things work together for good to those who love God, to those who are the called according to His purpose."
— Romans 8:28 (NKJV)

What are some things you admire and appreciate about your husband? Write here.

Conclusion

A sobering truth about marriage is that it is hard and requires work, but a more encouraging one is that it can be very beautiful! Nothing lasting is acquired easily. As my husband and I are helping our children that are *legally* young adults (because of age) transition into *actual* adulthood, we remind them of this all the time. People advise them to stay home, travel the world, acquire things and experiences that they've always wanted. We tell them that all of those things are in reach for them, as long as they will put in the work on the front end. If they first chase becoming responsible adults, and God's will for their lives, they can eventually travel and acquire whatever they want, and they will appreciate it all the more having worked for it. Marriage is similar in that the 'two becoming one' is more difficult at the beginning of the relationship. You have to put in the work, but as you go along, it gets easier. You will still face trials, but as you learn to stride together, you can deal with or endure them with more grace, and without big fall-outs.

I want to reiterate to you that no marriage is perfect. But to have a great marriage, you need two things:

- First, you need to acquire knowledge, and you're reading this book, so you already have an idea of this. Just know that you never stop learning, so continue on your quest for understanding.
- Then, you need to put the knowledge into action. This is the tricky part because no one can tell you precisely how to apply the knowledge in *your* marriage. I can only give ideas and examples. You will need to seek God in prayer, and surround yourself with other like-minded married women to put these truths to work in your life.

A summary of my prayer for you, once you have gotten to this page, is that this book has given you a more practical way of approaching your marriage, while still painting a picture of the beauty that is the marriage relationship, and that you will trust God and put these principles to work in your relationship with your husband!

"If any of you lacks wisdom, let him ask God, who gives generously to all without reproach, and it will be given him."

— James 1:5 (ESV)

"Oh, taste and see that the Lord is good! Blessed is the man who takes refuge in him!"
— Psalm 34:8 (ESV)

Reflections

Now that you've read all that I have shared with you in this book, write down some ways you can be proactive in building your marriage relationship.

What have you learned about yourself, your husband or your marriage while reading this book? Write about it here.

Appendix:
A List of Other Resources

I have included some practical resources for you to tap into, as you continue your journey of building a healthy marriage:

A. **TriMarriage.com**
Our website will connect you with our blog as well as our social media pages for regular encouragement, guidance and instruction.

B. **The Marriage Test**, a tool designed to bring to light specific areas in your marriage that need your attention, and start you on your way to addressing them is on the TriMarriage website. You can click on the "Resources" tab or go to this address:
https://www.trimarriage.com/resources-1

C. **The Ten Rules of Marital Warfare** can also be found on TriMarriage.com, on the "Resources" tab or at the address above.

D. **Revive Our Hearts 30-Day Husband Encouragement Challenge:**
https://www.reviveourhearts.com/articles/30-day-husband-encouragement-challenge/

E. **Revive Our Hearts 30-Day Praying For Your Husband Challenge:**
https://www.reviveourhearts.com/articles/31-days-of-praying-for-your-husband/

F. **iamhisgoodthing.com**
I Am His Good Thing is a ministry, based off Proverbs 18:22, to wives and women who desire marriage. The ministry mission is to draw women back into intimacy with Jesus Christ by equipping and encouraging them with biblical tools, community, and content so they grow closer to God and their husband.

G. **Linda Dillow and Dr. Juli Slattery *Passion Pursuit: What Kind of Love Are You Making?* Chicago: Moody, 2013**

H. *Gary Chapman (1992) The Five Love Languages: How to Express Heartfelt Commitment to Your Mate. Northfield Publishing*

Acknowledgements

To my husband Anthony... my lover who loves me like Christ loved the Church — Not perfectly, but about as close as I've seen. You have shown me what unconditional love actually looks like, and taught me how to reciprocate it. It is through our relationship that I have come to appreciate and understand so much about the importance of the wife's role as described in the Bible. God used the way that you love me as a template to help me start to grasp the depth of His love for me. It is from this understanding that I find the strength to push forward, and do what God has ordained for me to do. Our marriage relationship has made me a better wife, mother, daughter, sister, friend, and total woman of God. I love you forever!

Jamaya: We have been journeying side by side, on separate projects, but mirroring in progress! I appreciate our conversations as we encourage one another to move forward with patience or wisdom, or whatever we needed at the time! You inspire me as I watch you diligently chase God, and the dreams He put on your heart. Go get'em, girl!

Kelly P. for all of your advice and encouragement, and for being an inspiration to me!

Kelly and Nichelle: You guys were the first to point out to me that I had something to share that could help women in their marriages! You both have continued to encourage me in this. I love you both, and thank you!

To my parents, Melvin and Marilyn Murphy who raised me according to the grace and knowledge of my Lord and Savior Jesus Christ. They prayed for me in secret, and were the first to perceive that my walk with Christ could impact His Kingdom for good. They believed that anyone who had a relationship with Christ could understand the Bible well enough to teach somebody something about what it says, so they put me and my younger sister in the rotation of teaching the family Bible study when we were still in elementary school! Daddy, I miss you so much, but I know that I will see you again when I leave this earth! I want you both to know that I listened to all the good stuff you tried to teach me growing up. The Lord just had to work it all out in my life! You did a good job! ♡

www.ingramcontent.com/pod-product-compliance
Ingram Content Group UK Ltd.
Pitfield, Milton Keynes, MK11 3LW, UK
UKHW020225250726
13967UKWH00001B/185

9 781638 776208